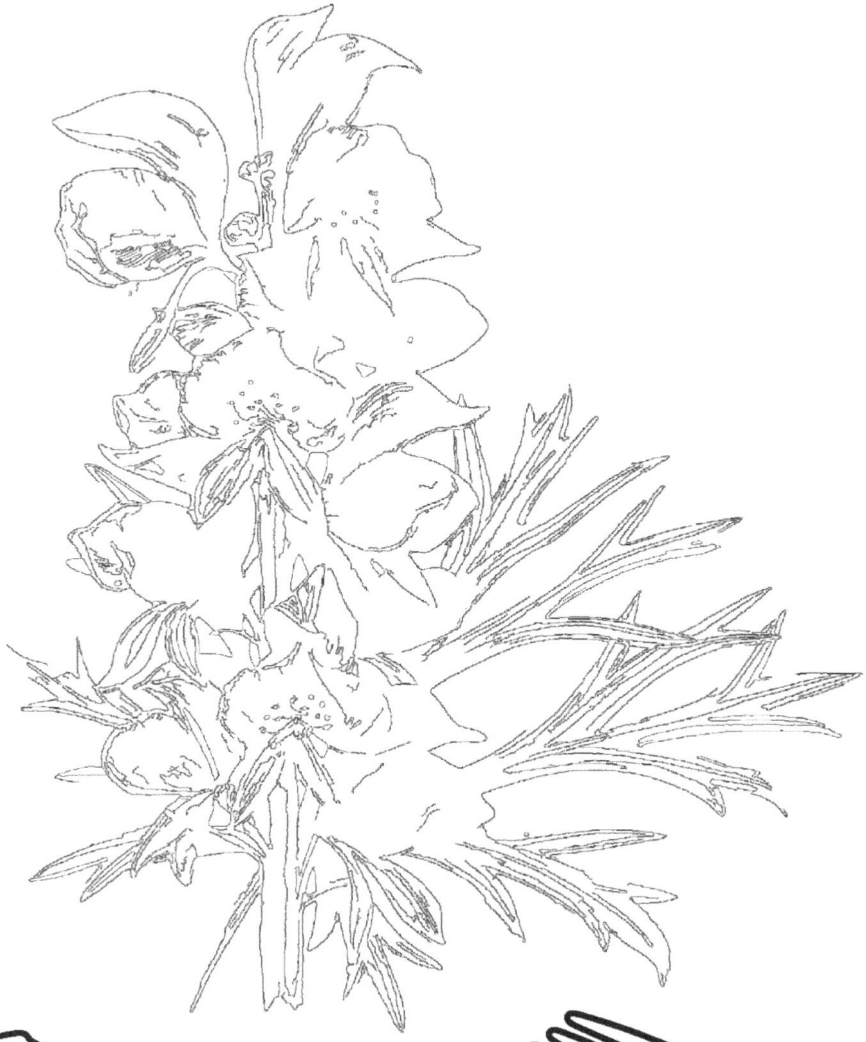

Enjoy Coloring!!!...

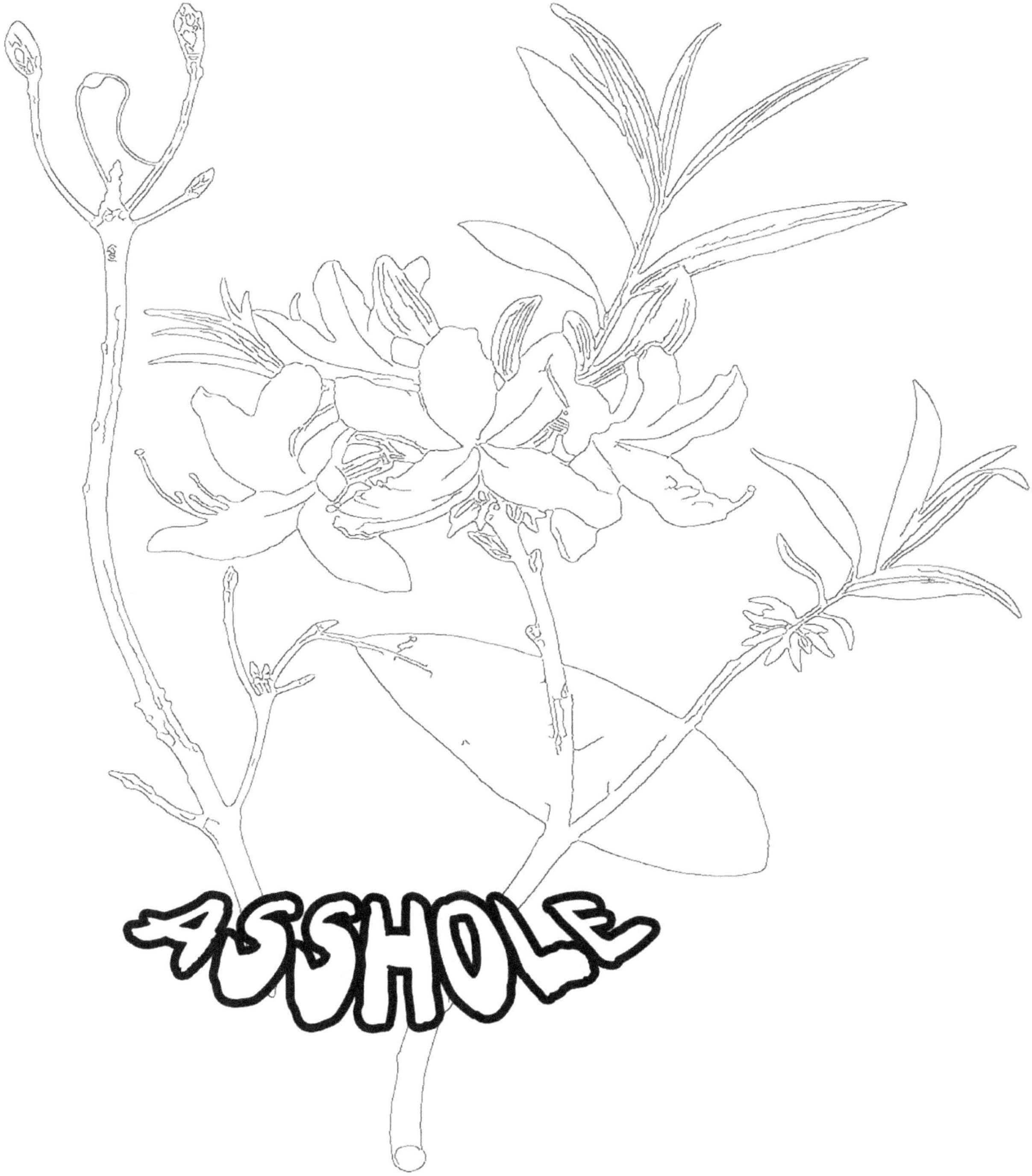
ASSHOLE

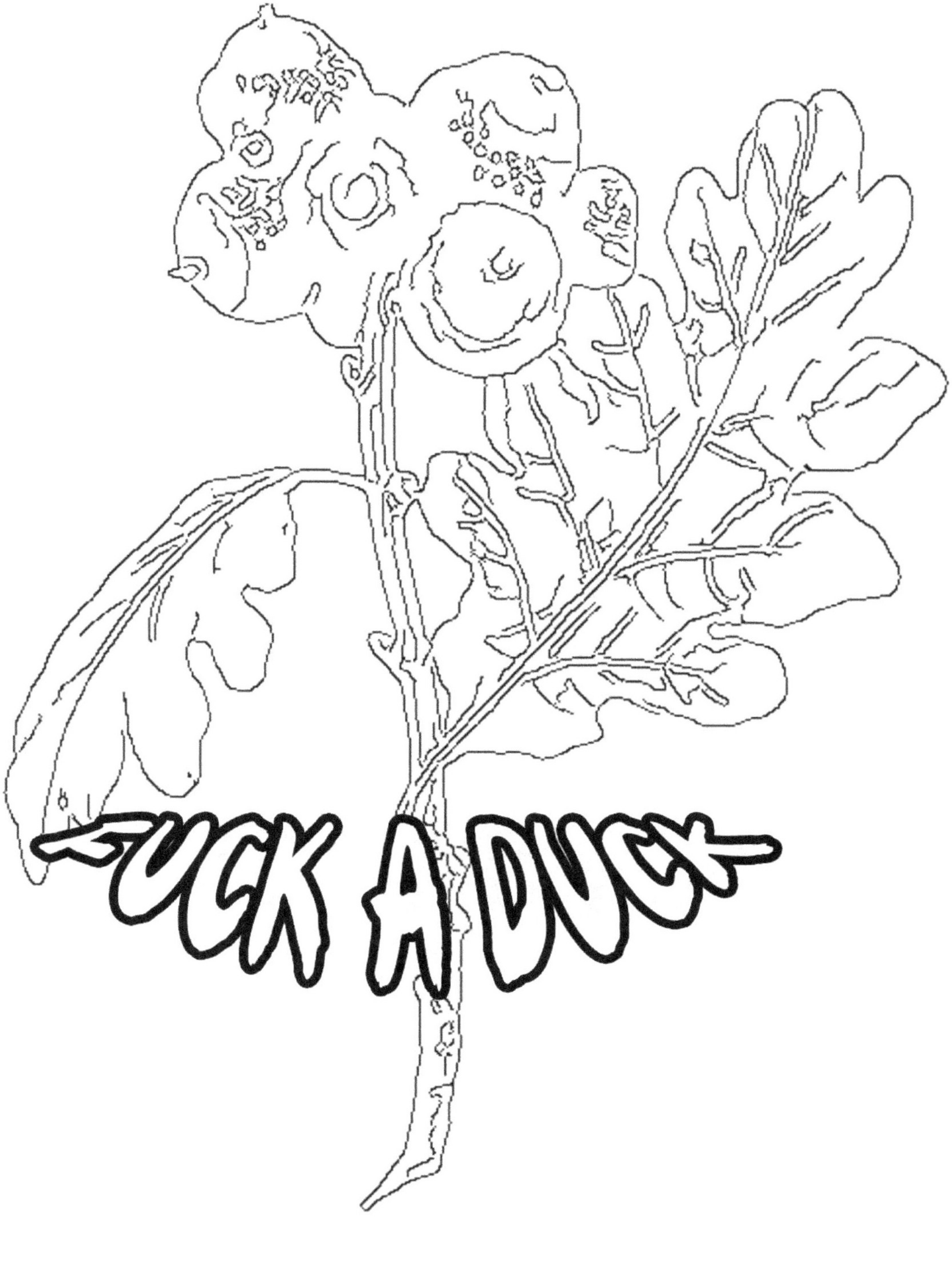
FUCK A DUCK

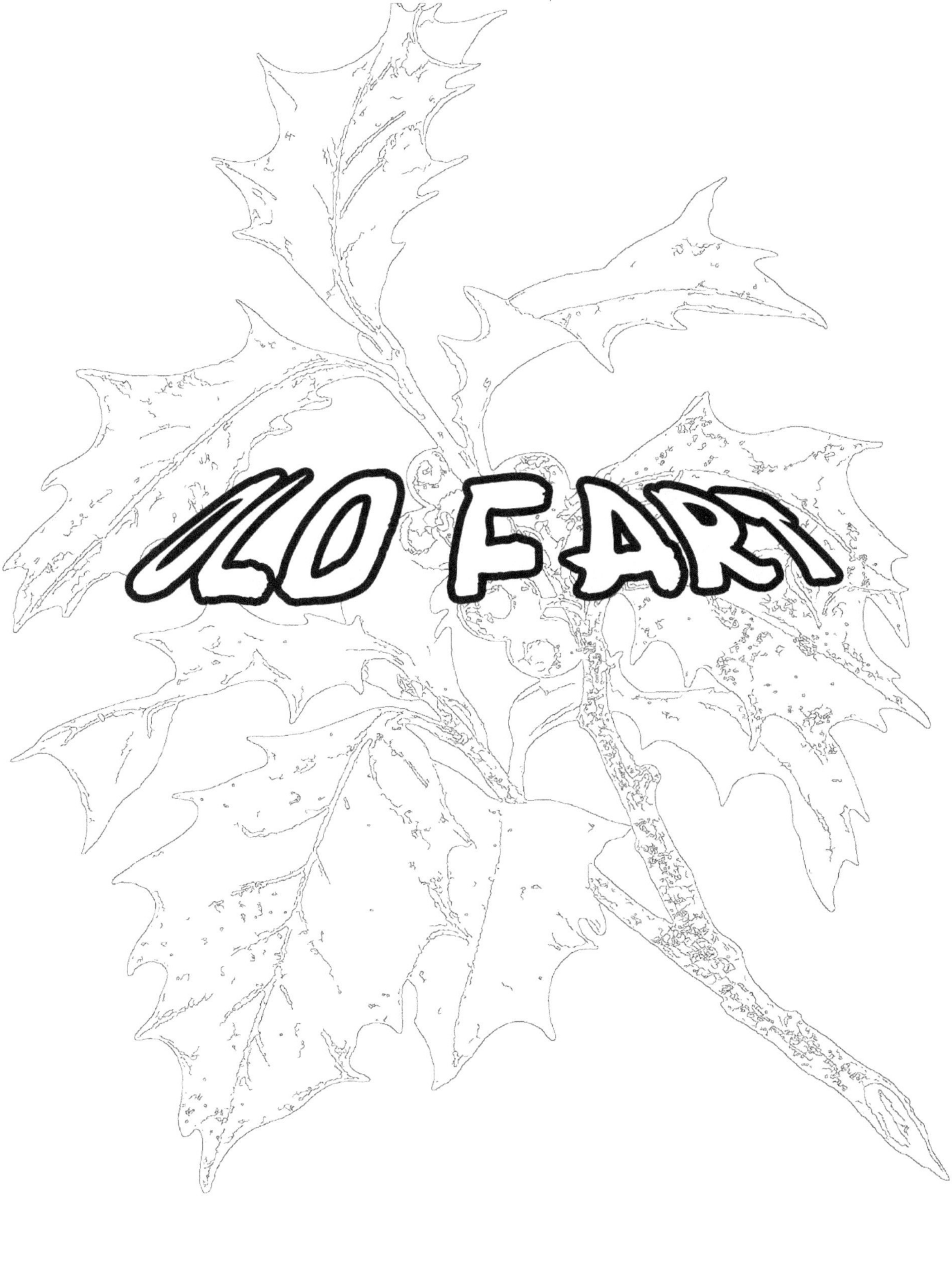
ILO F ART

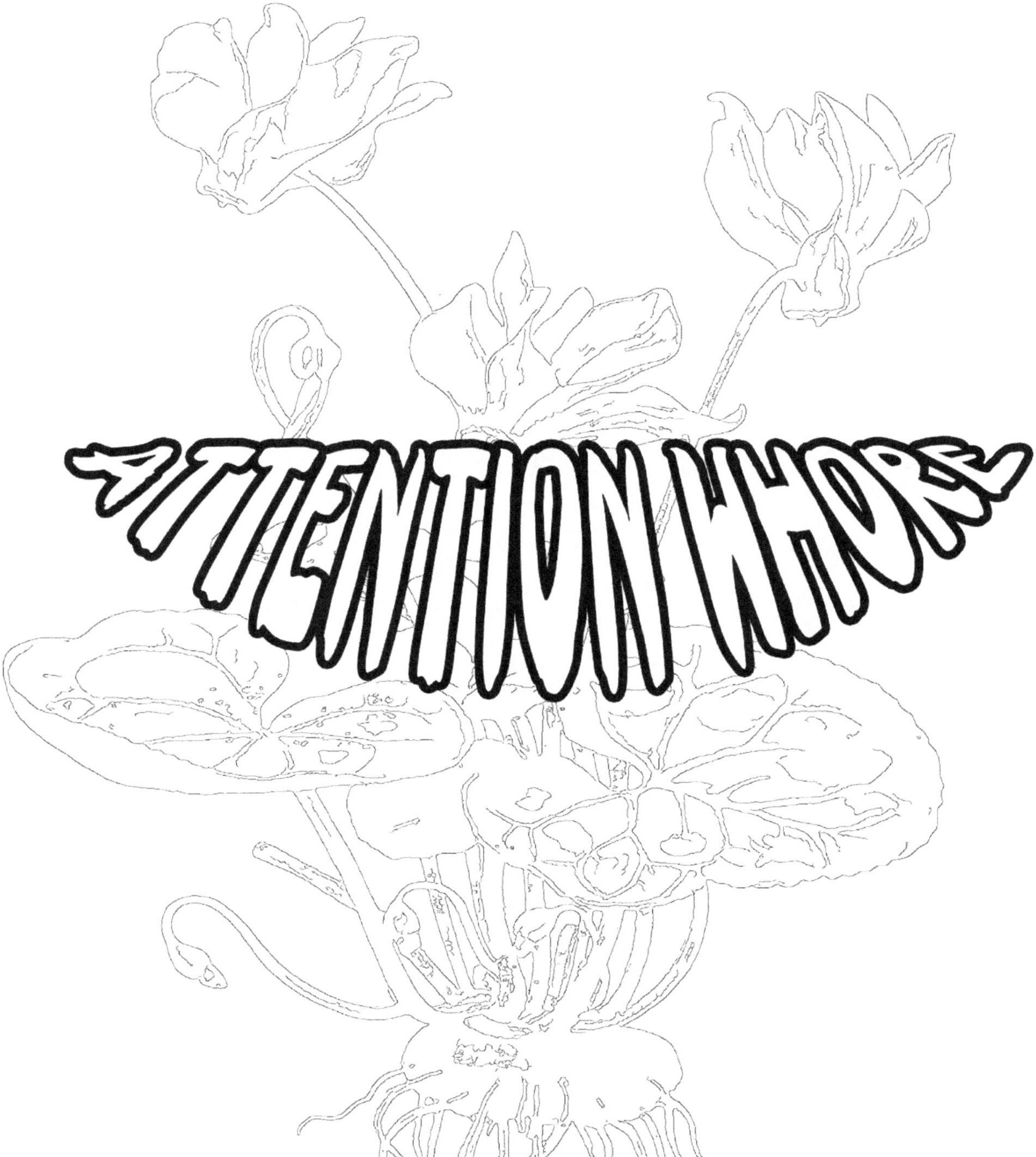
ATTENTION WHORE

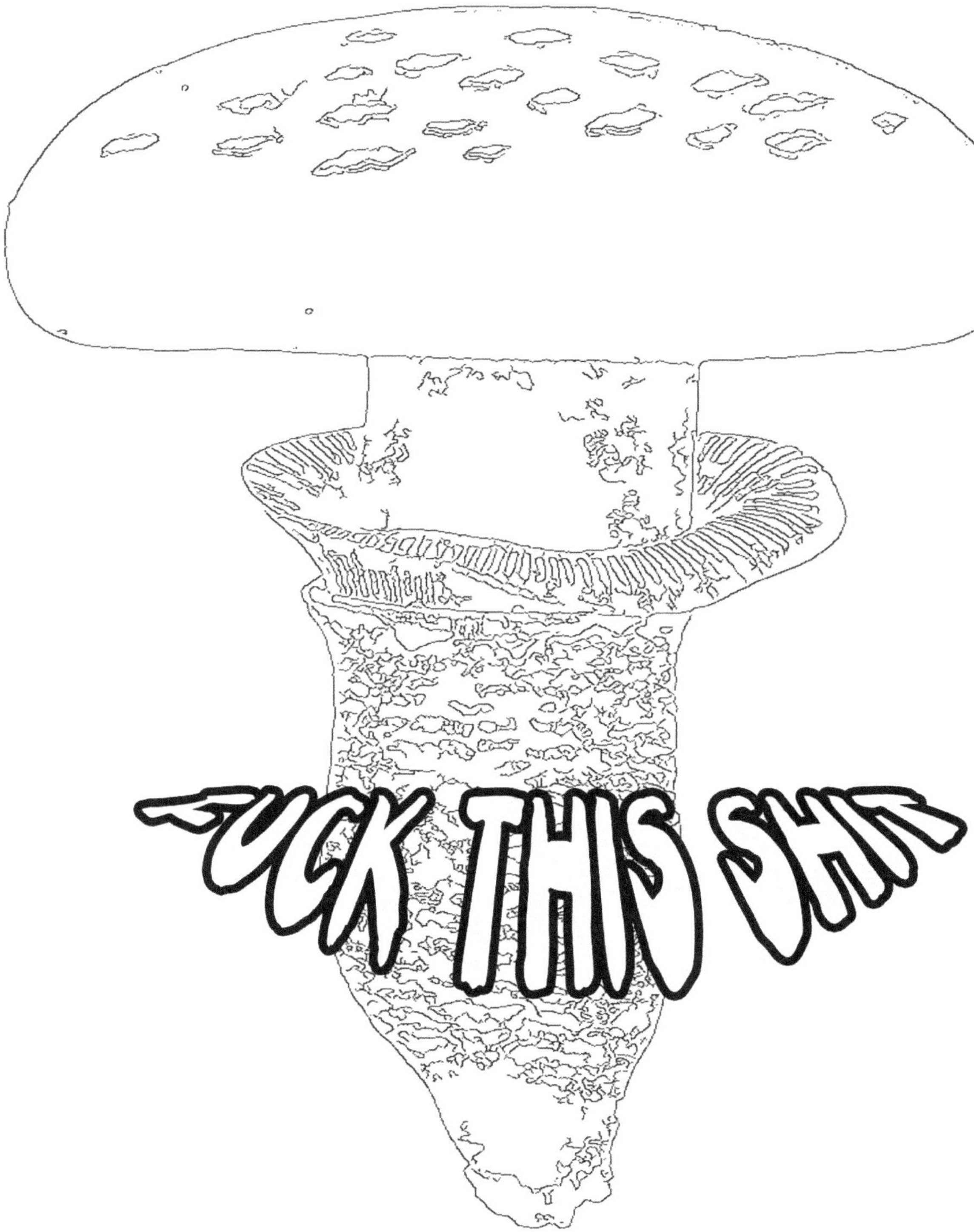
FUCK THIS SHIT

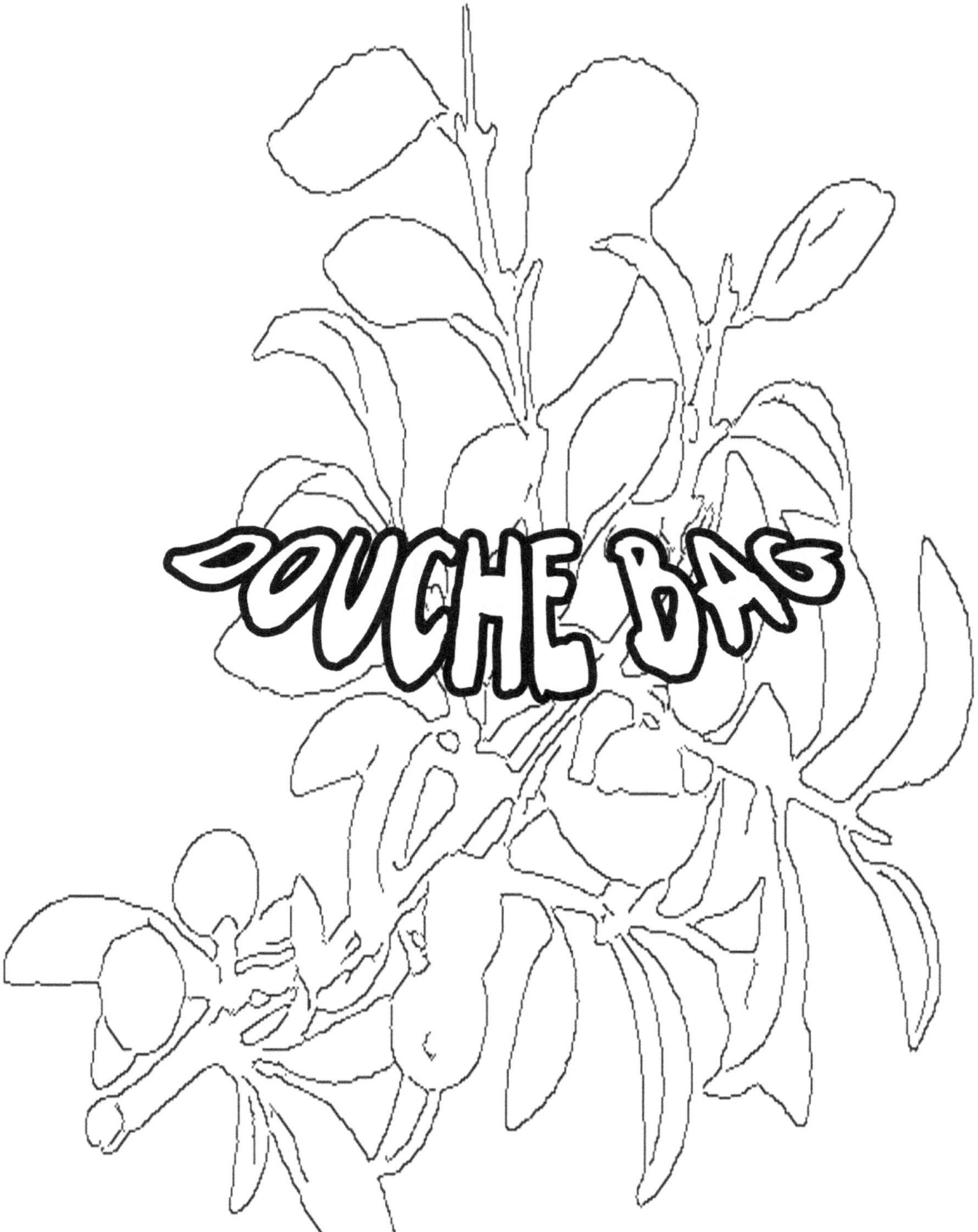
DOUCHE BAG

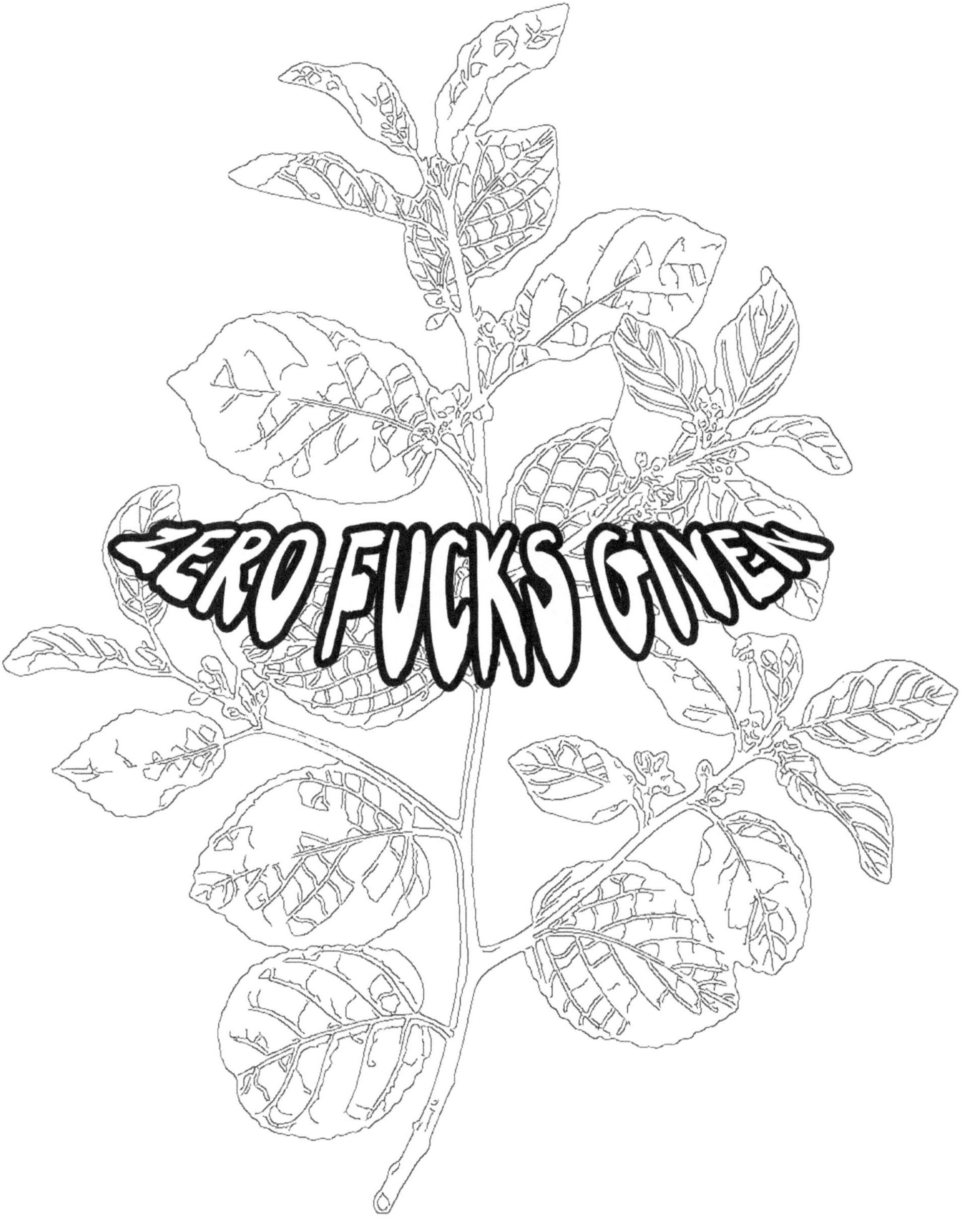
ZERO FUCKS GIVEN

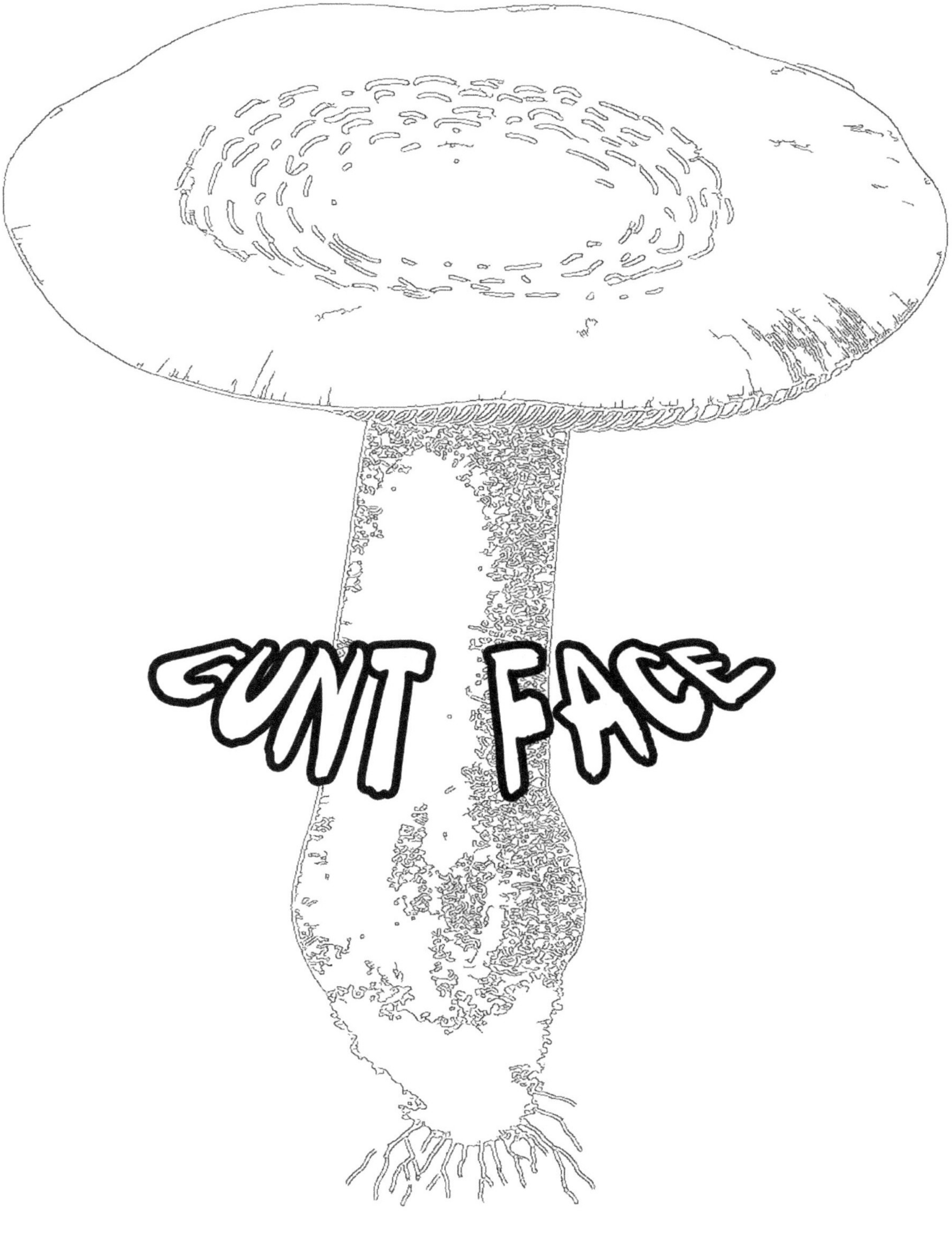
CUNT FACE

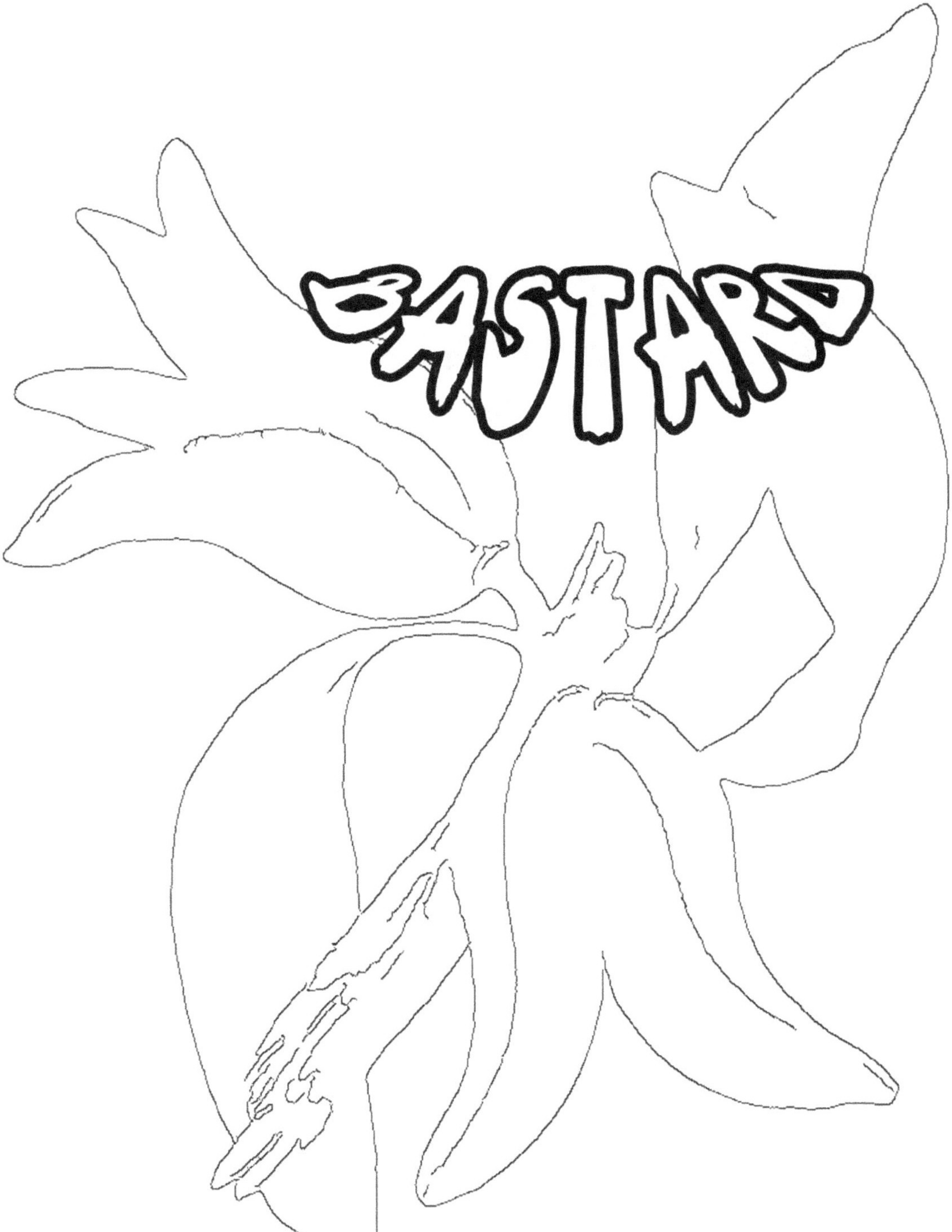
BASTARD

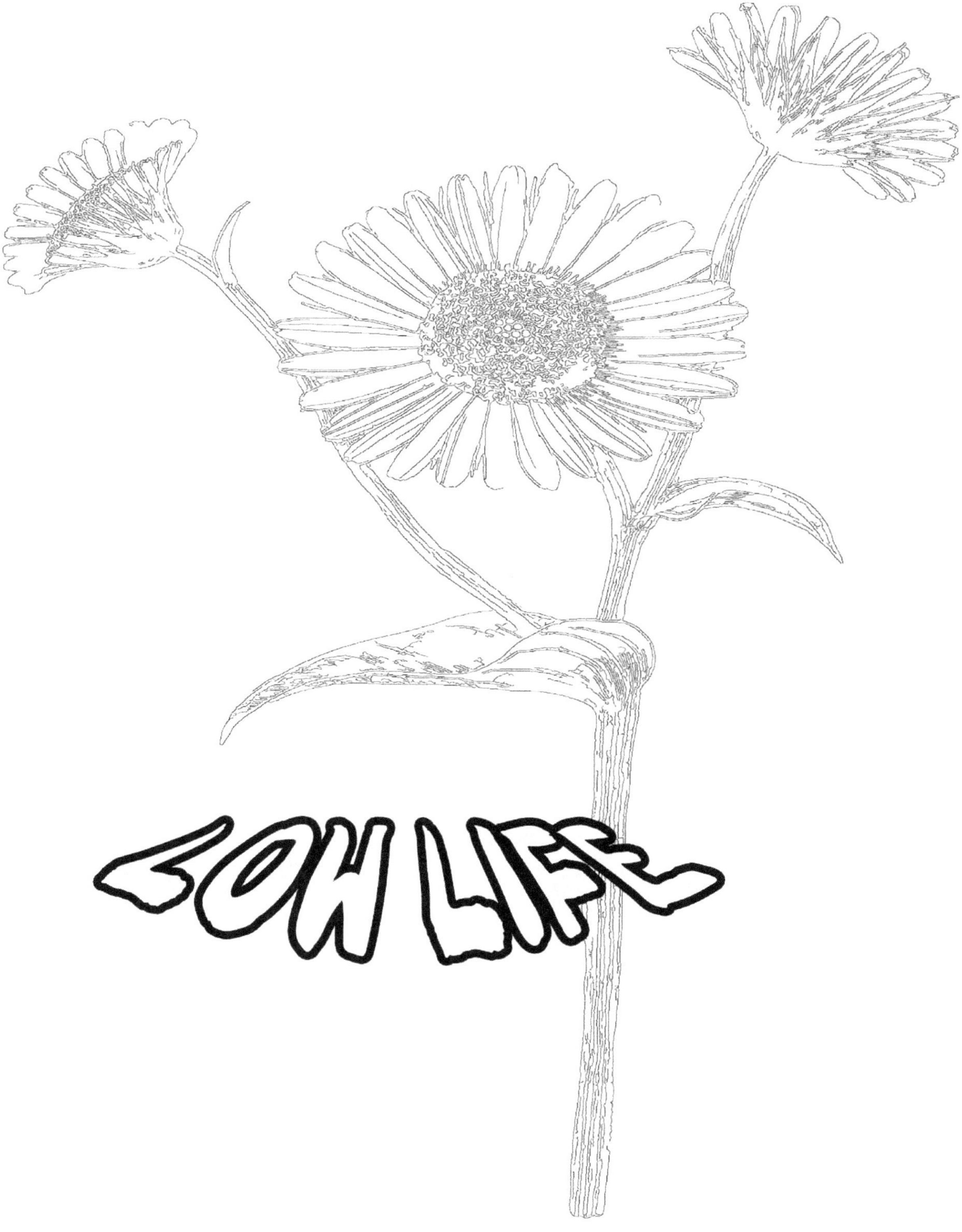
LOW LIFE

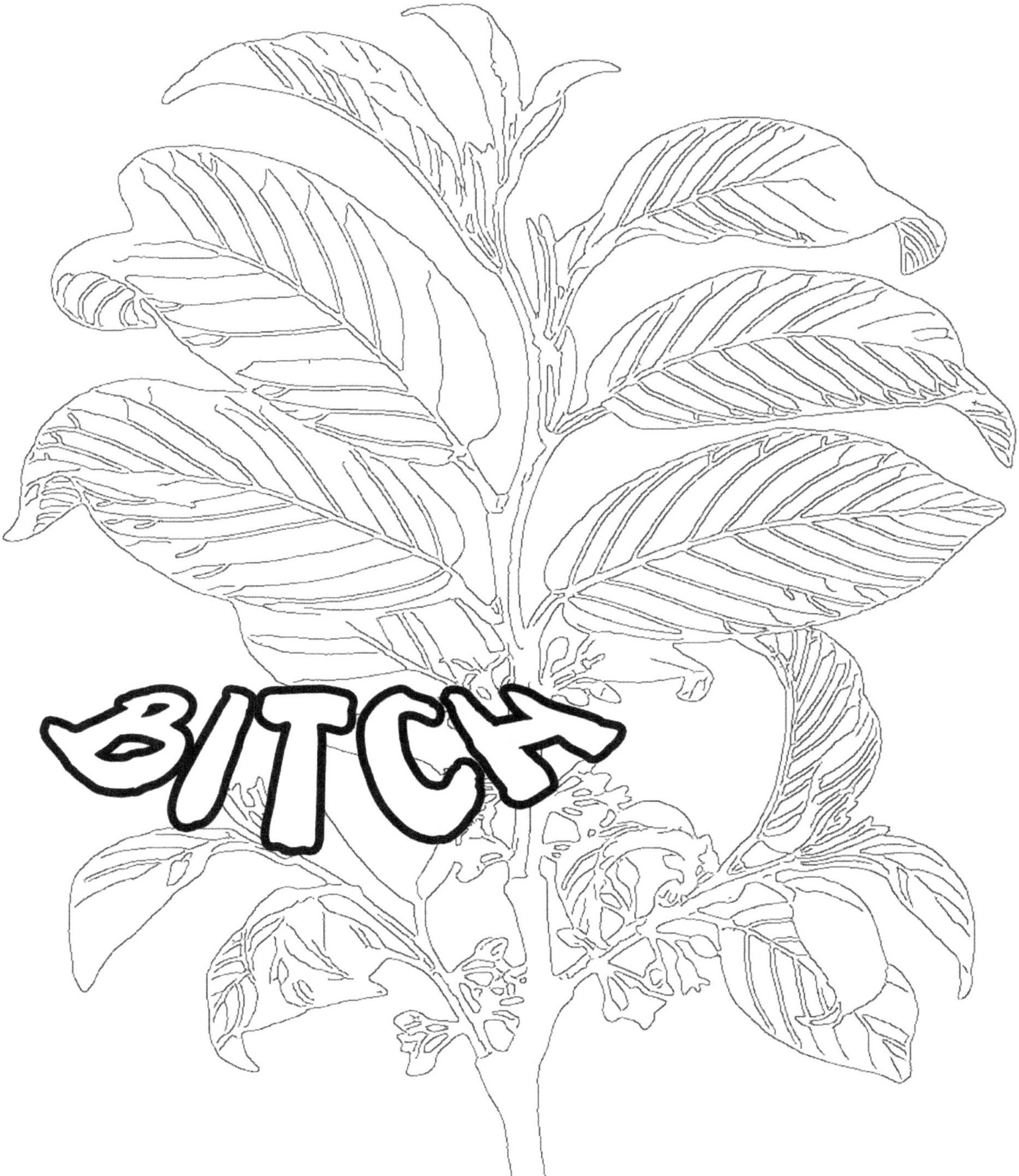
BITCH

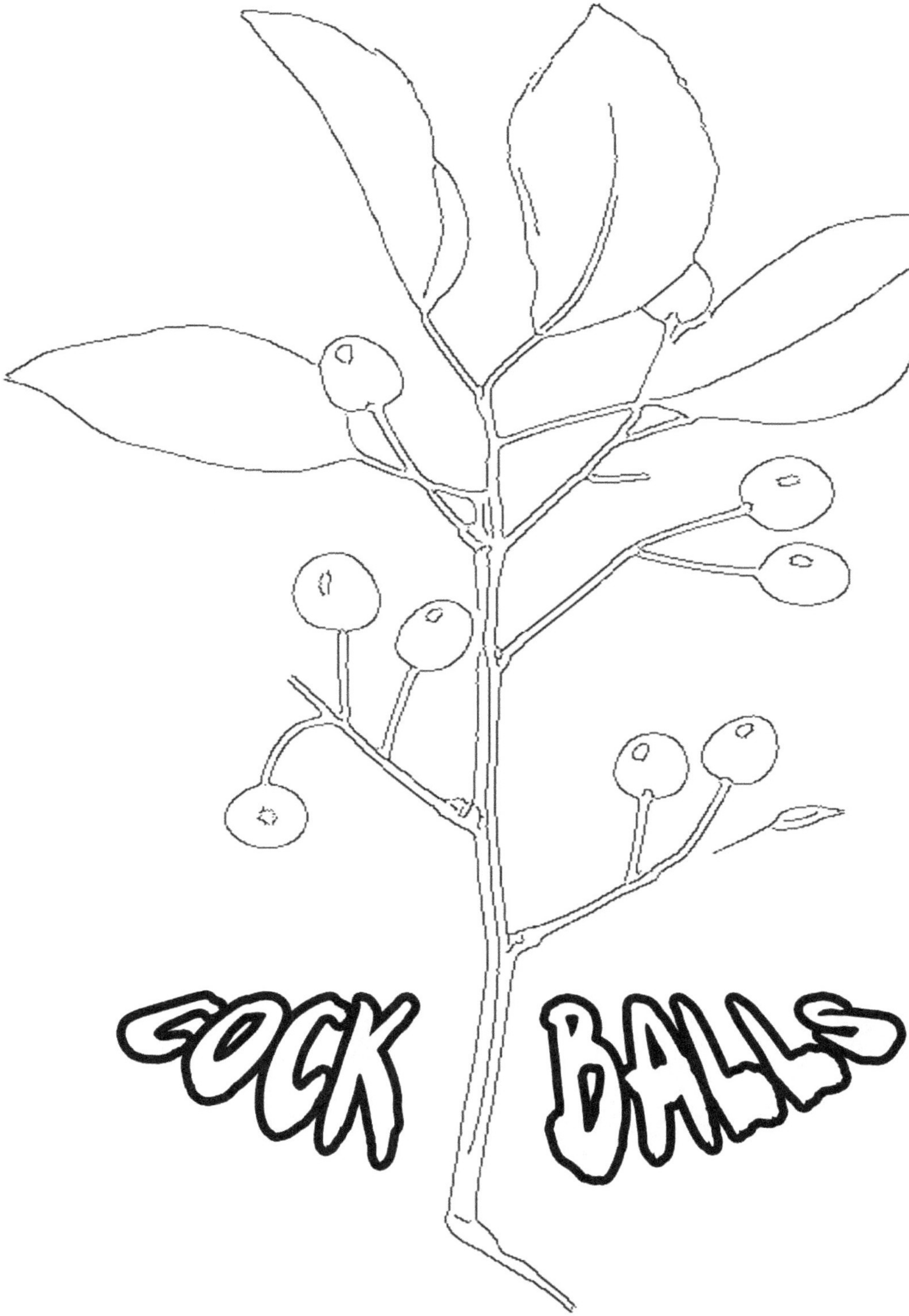
COCK
BALLS

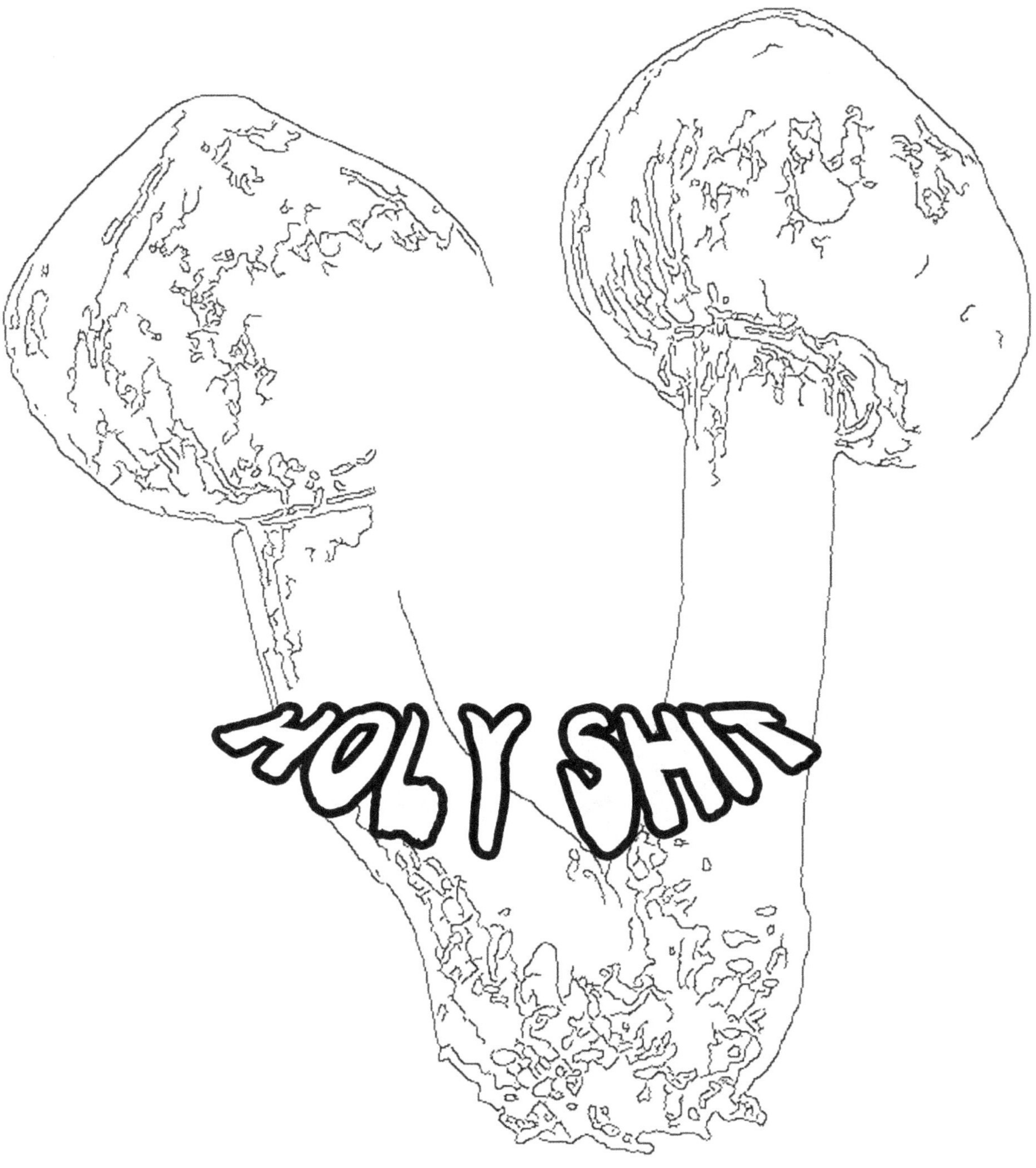
HOLY SHIT

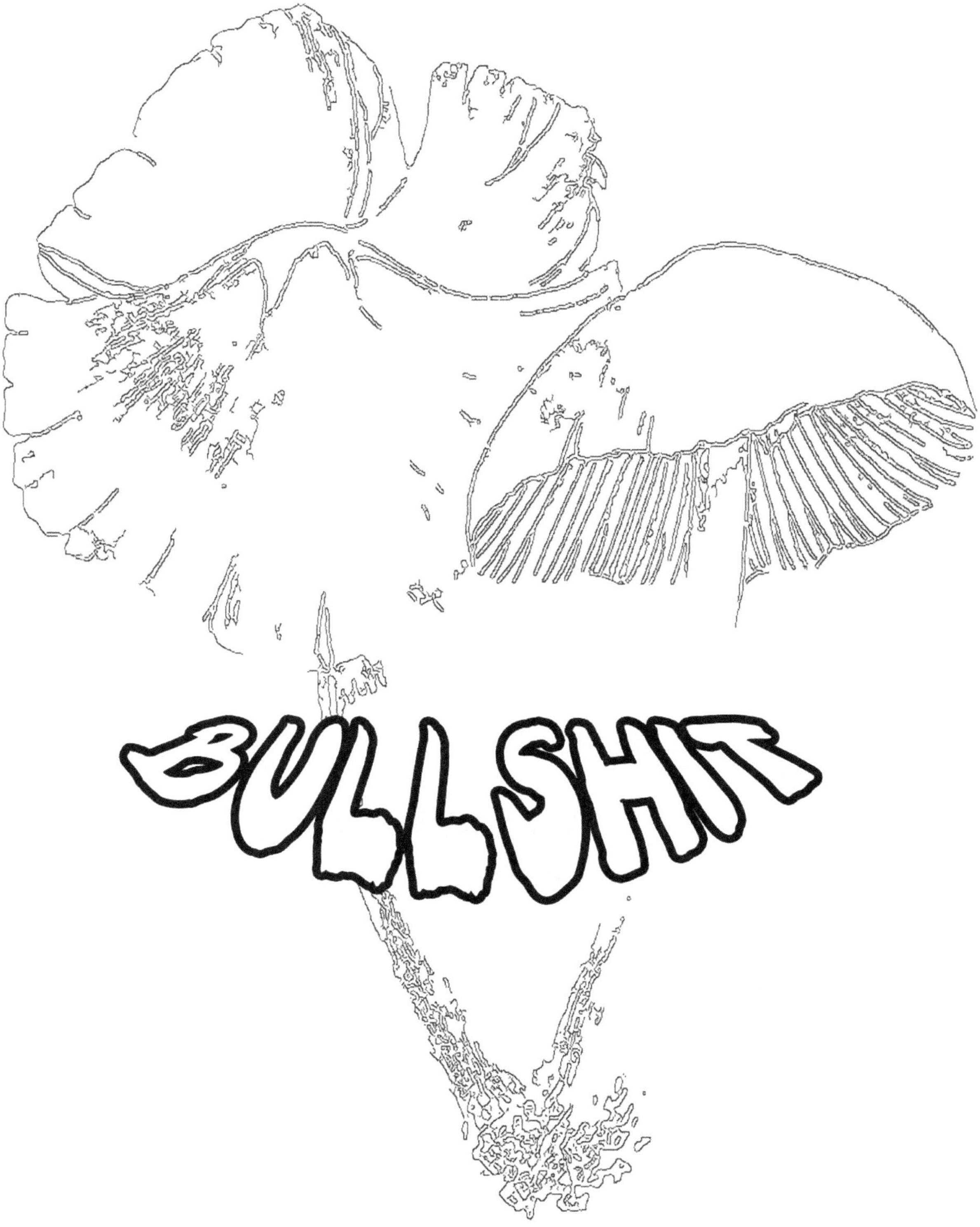
BULLSHIT

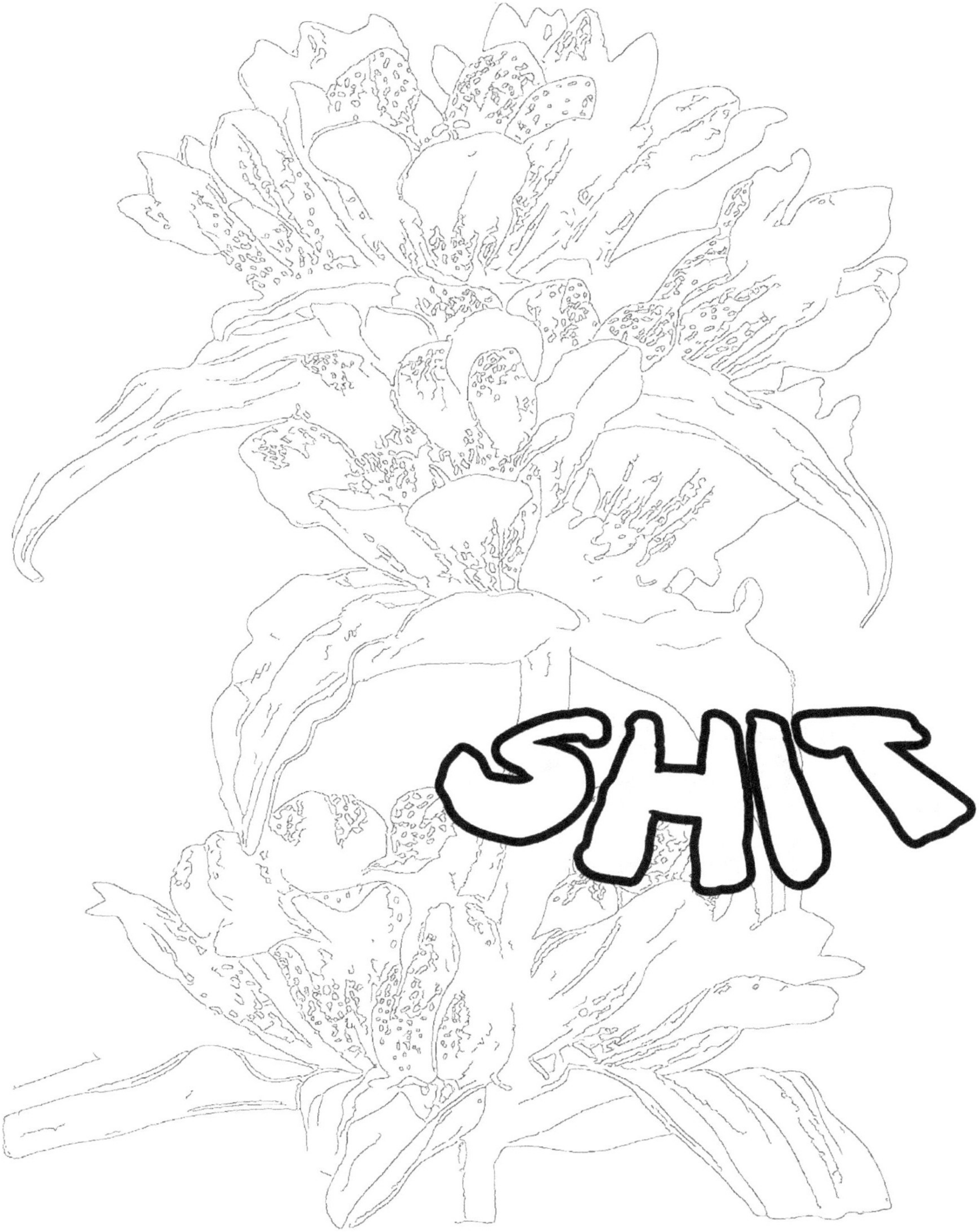
SHIT

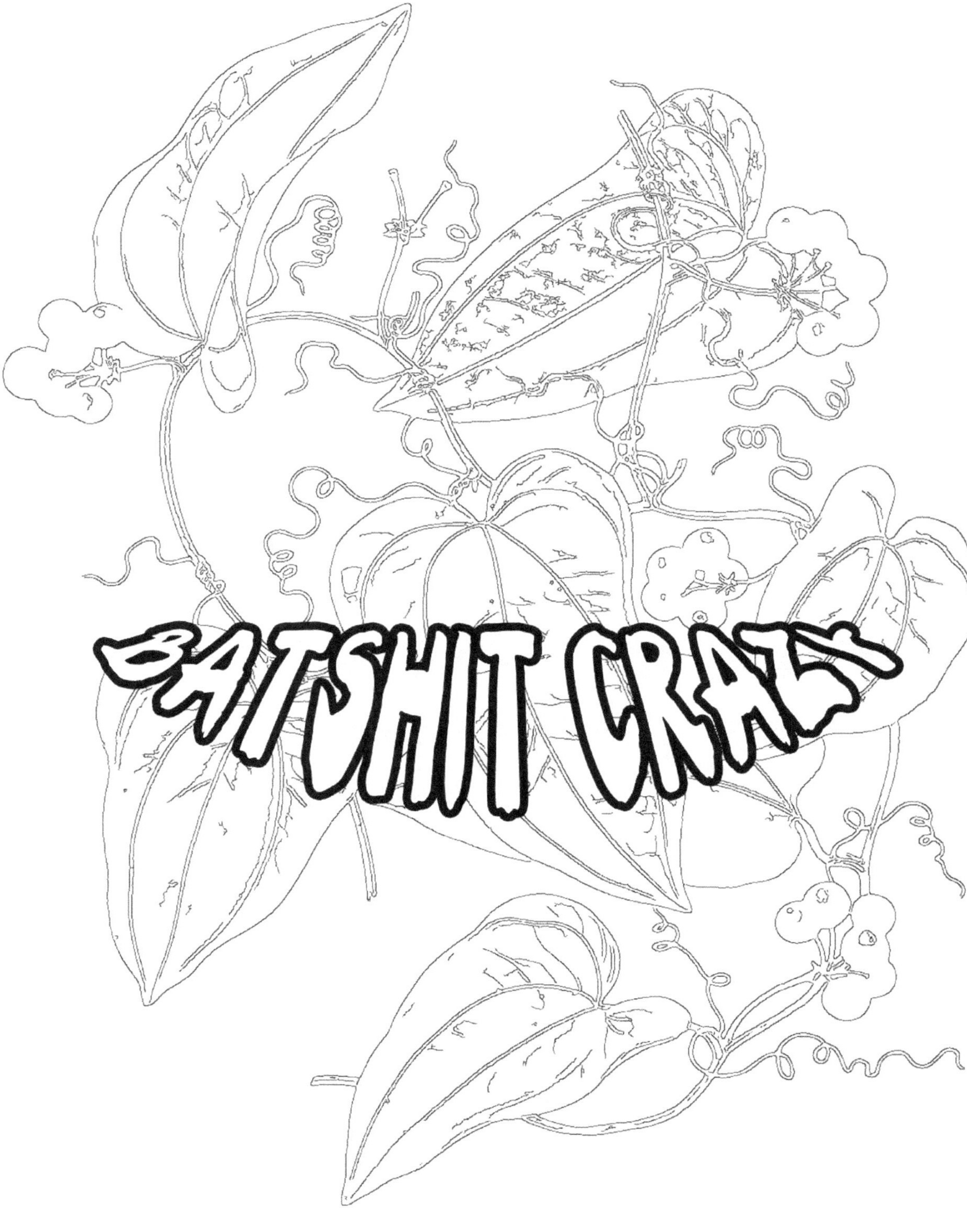
BATSHIT CRAZY

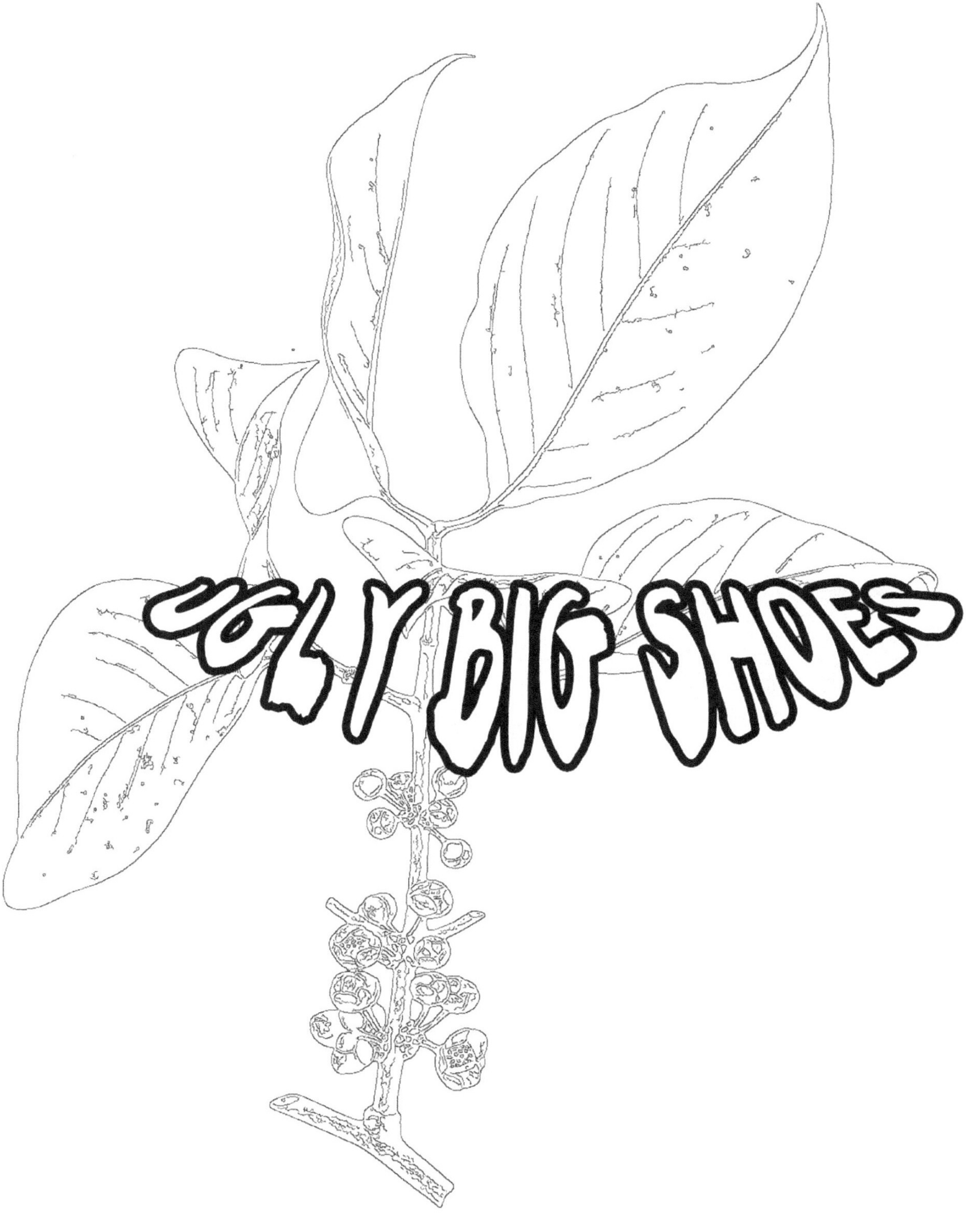
UGLY BIG SHOES

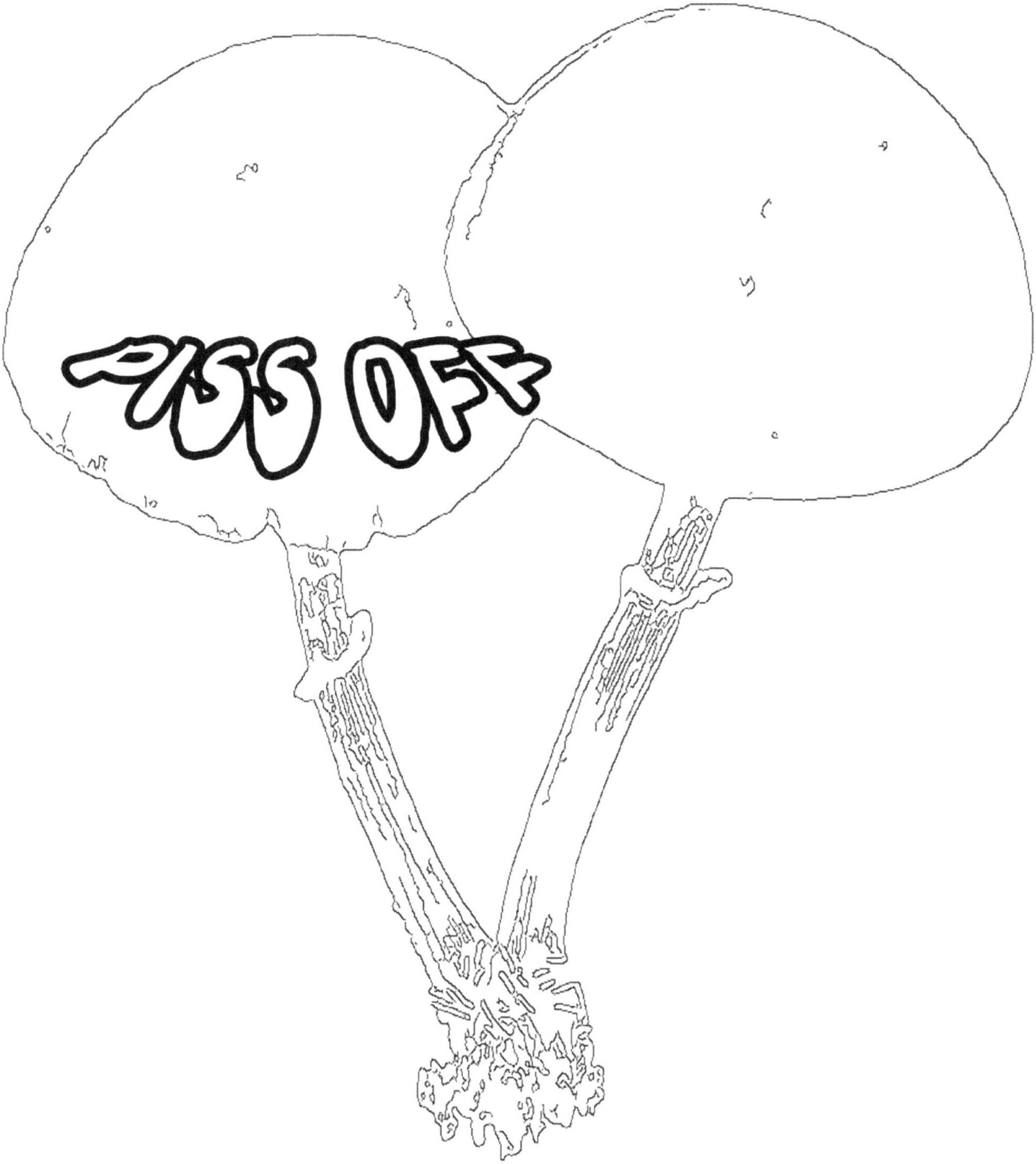
PISS OFF

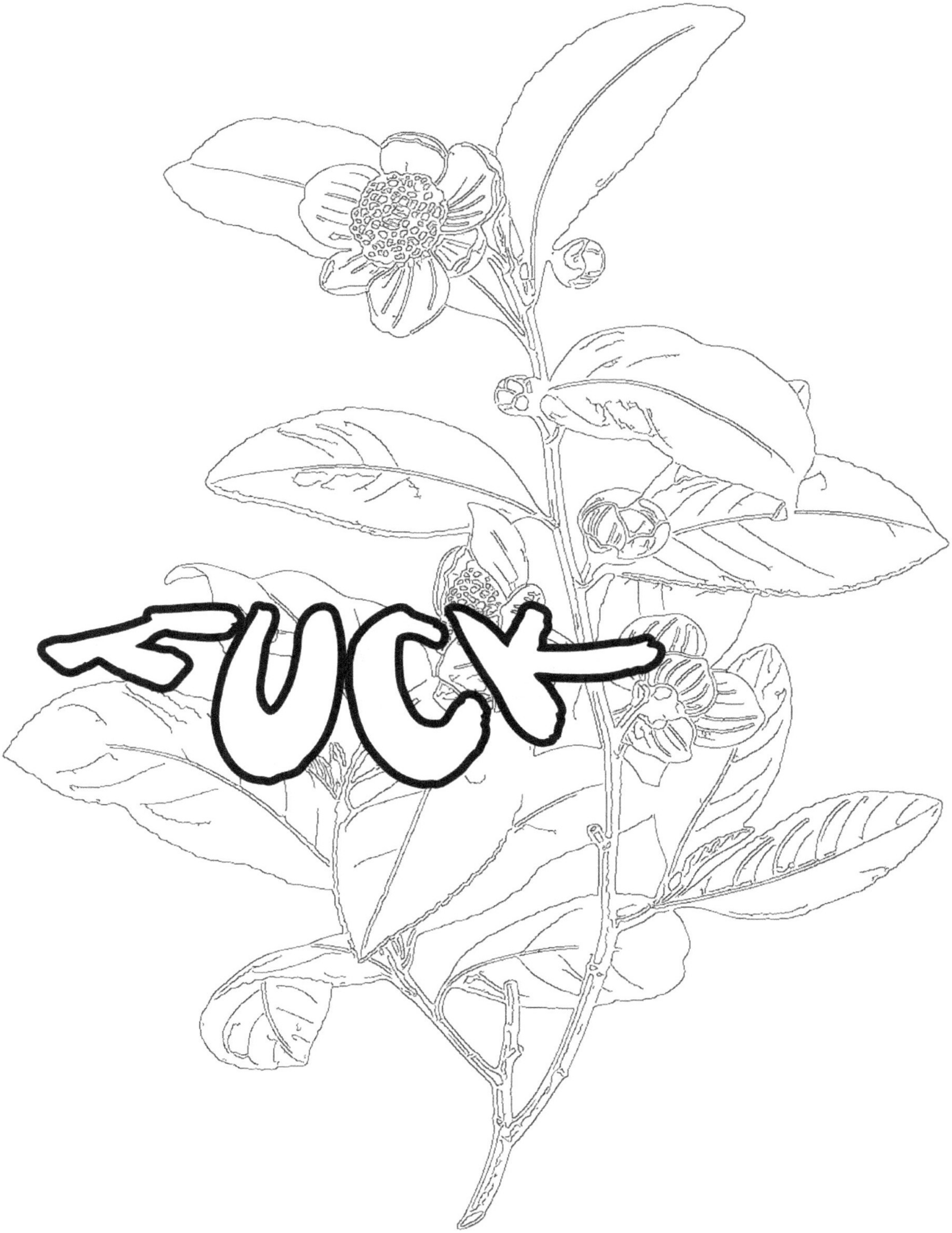
FUCK

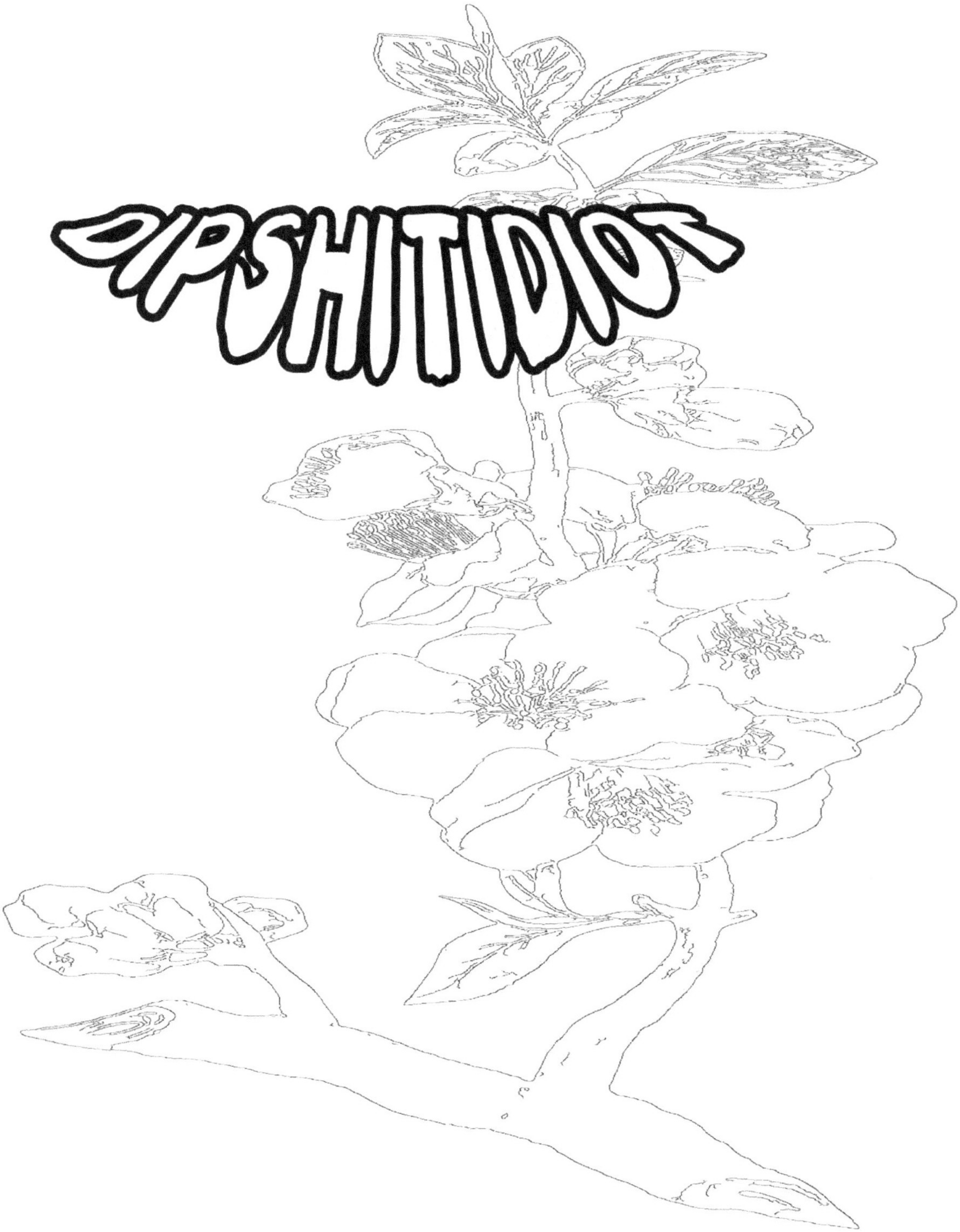
DIPSHITIDIOT

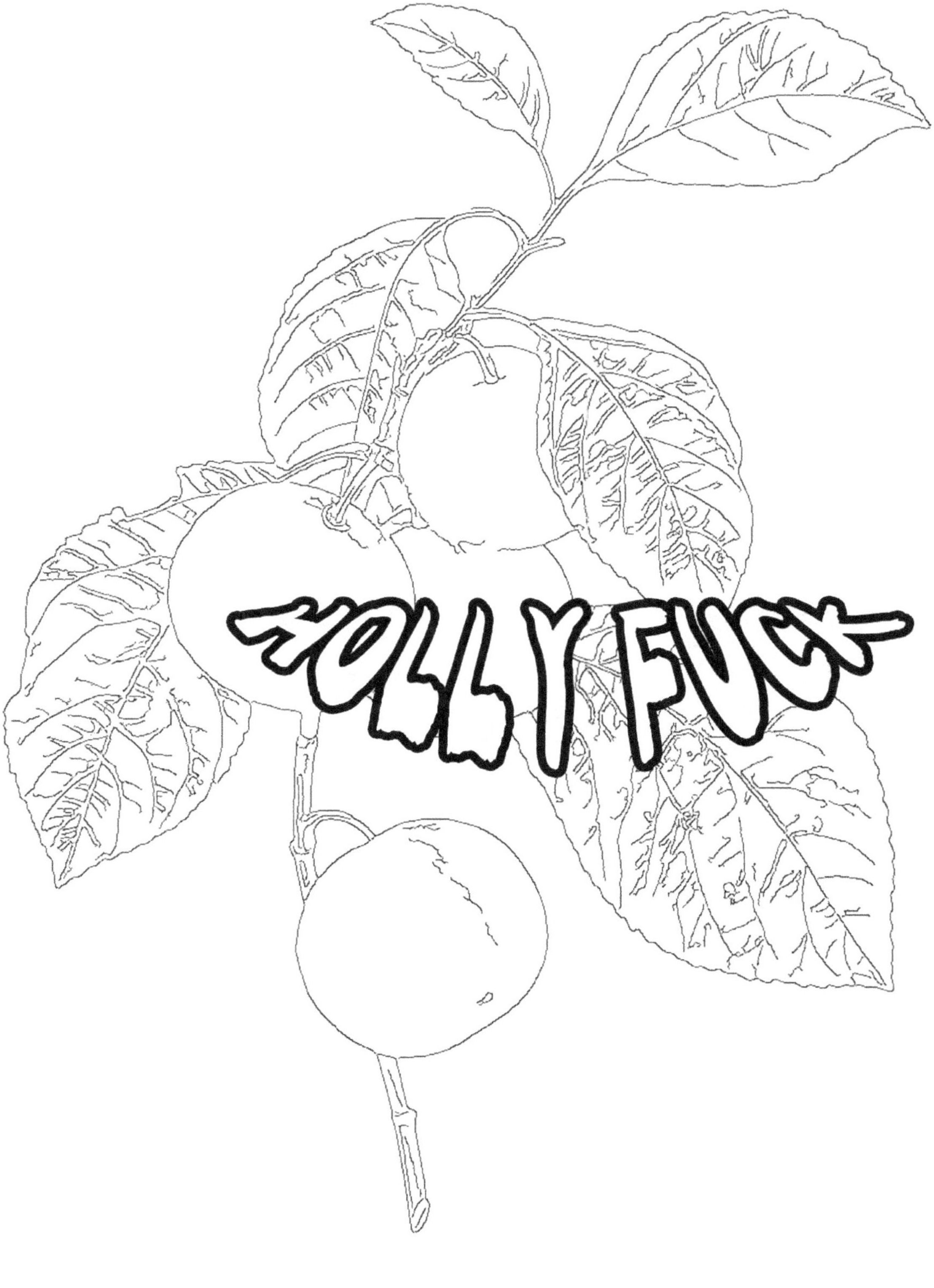
HOLLY FUCK

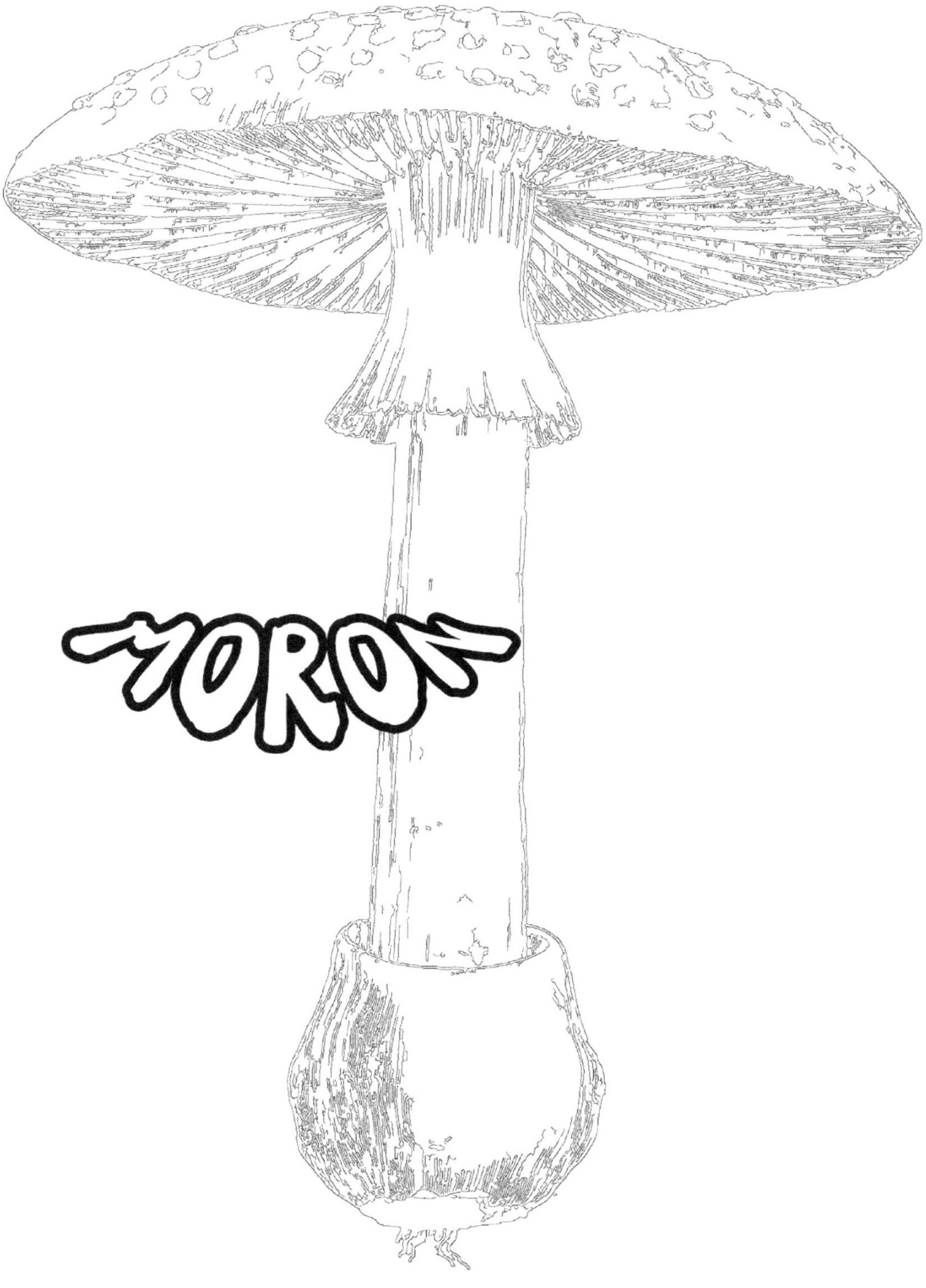
MORON

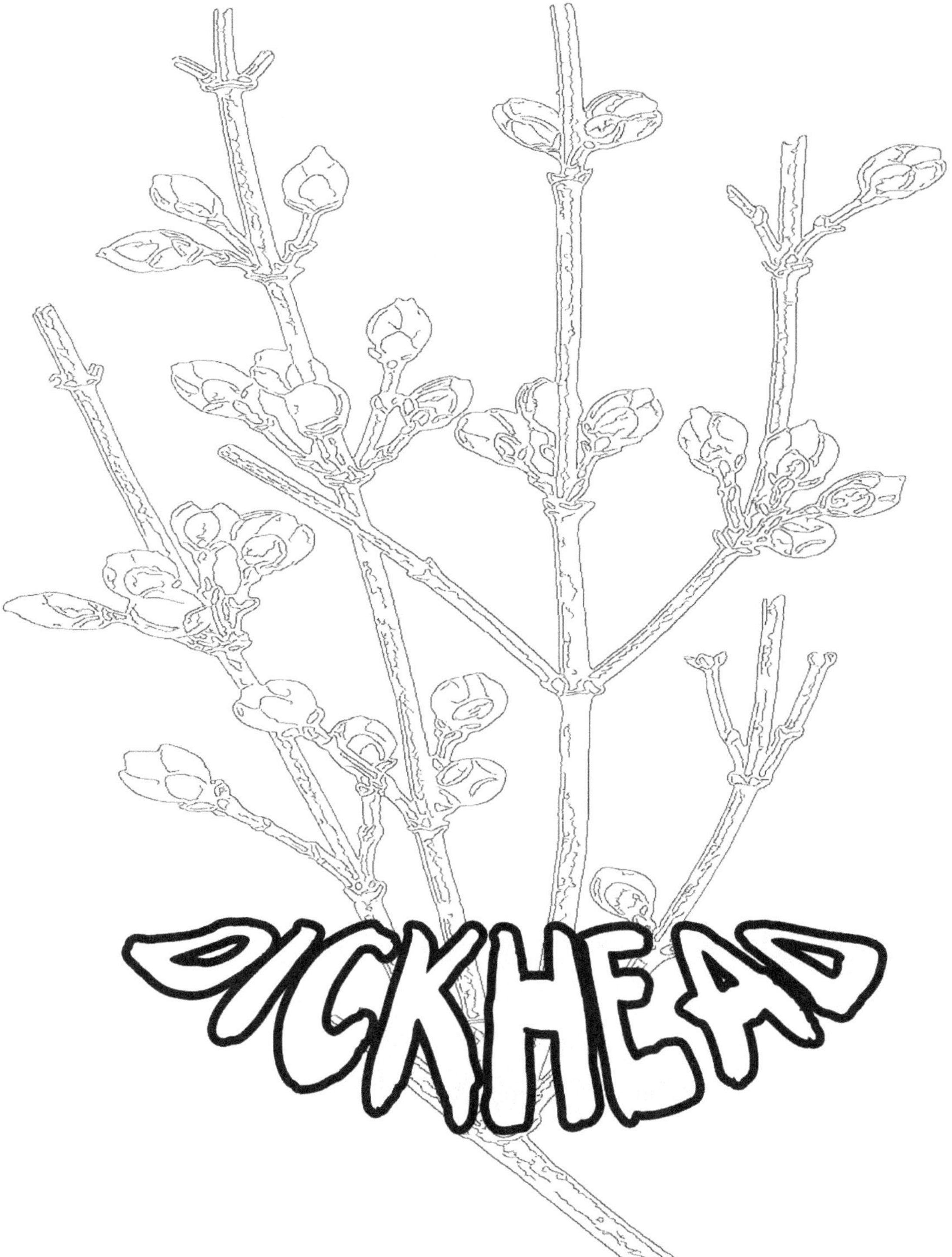
DICKHEAD

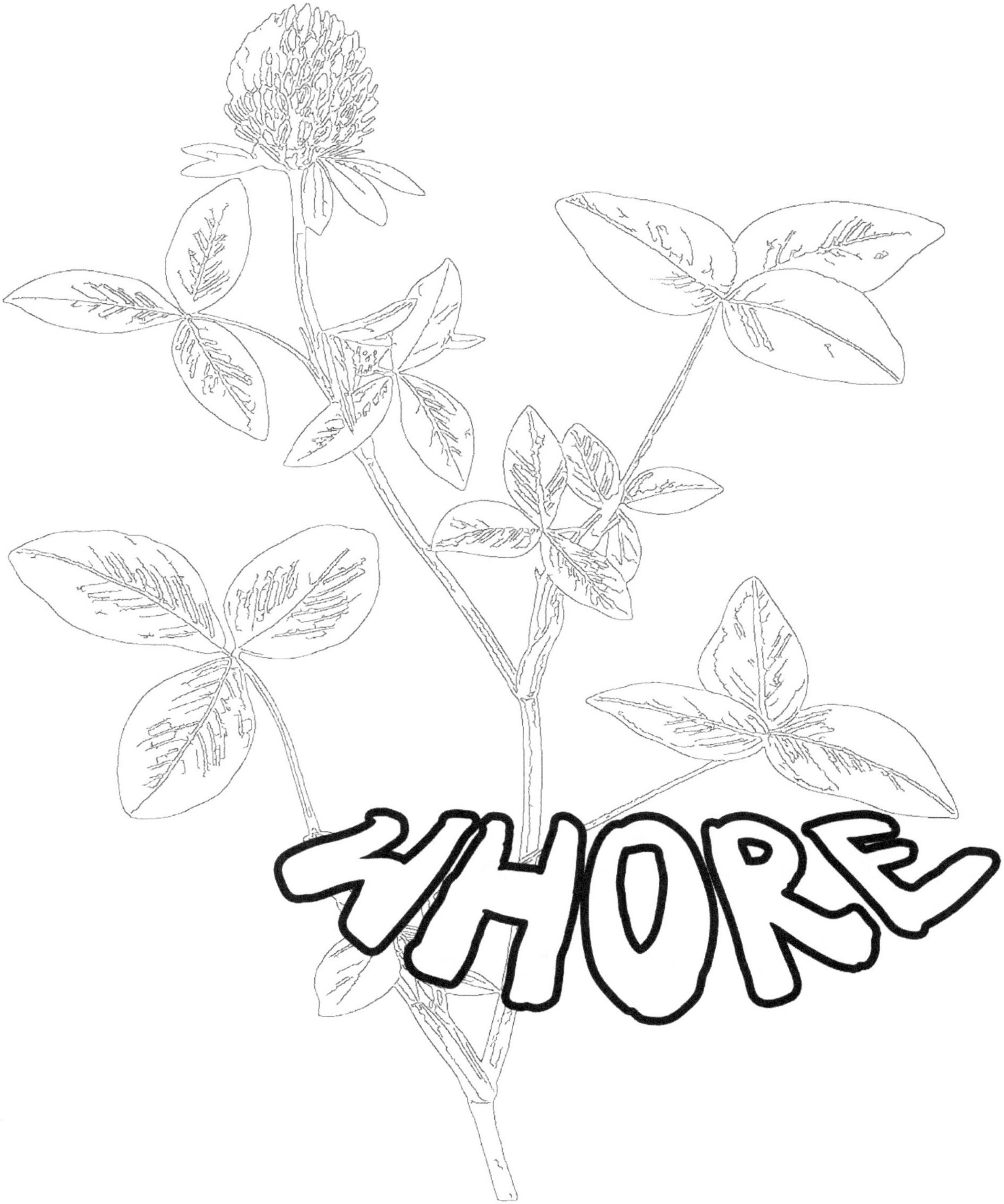
WHORE

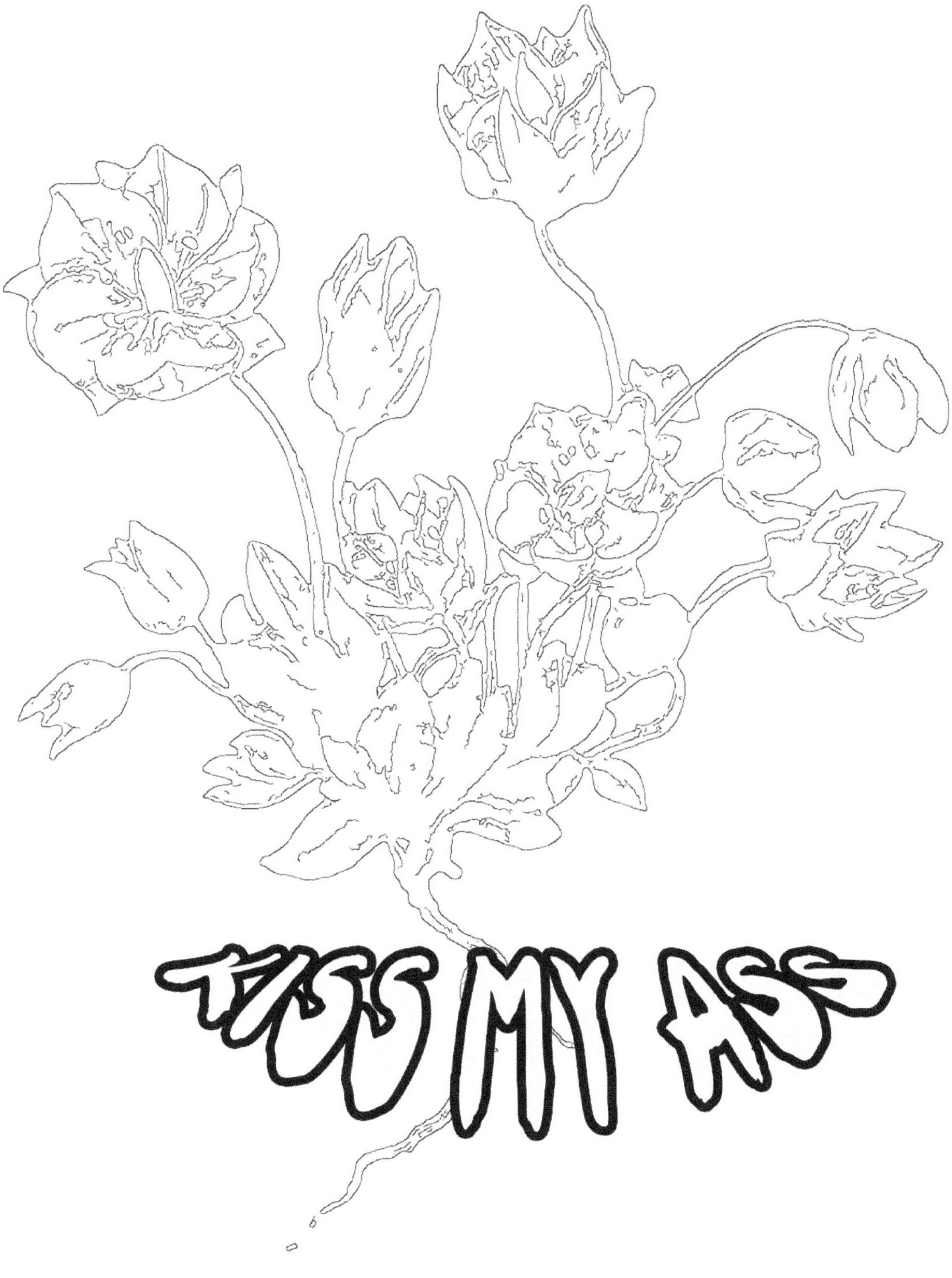
KISS MY ASS

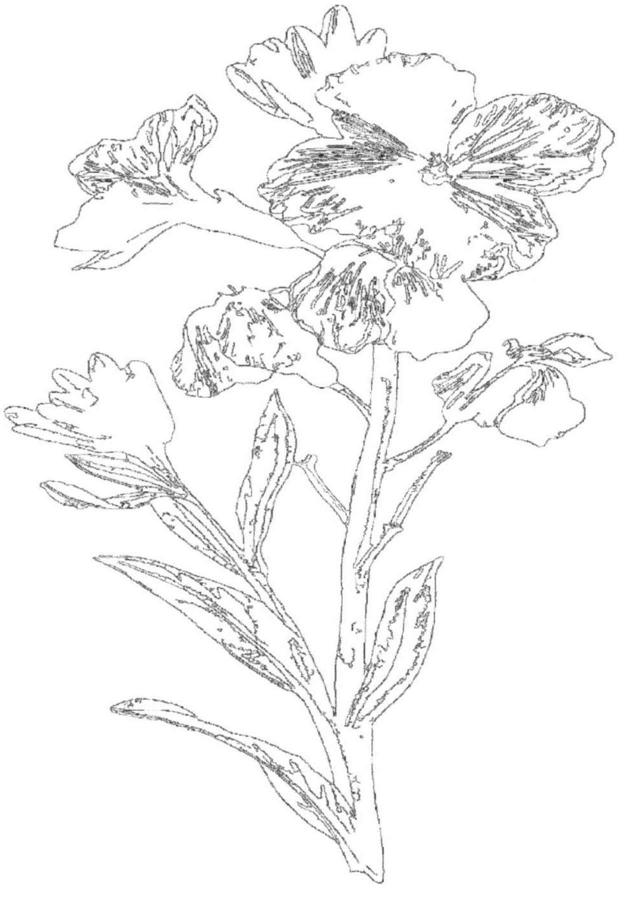

Have a good day.

www.ingramcontent.com/pod-product-compliance
Lightning Source LLC
Chambersburg PA
CBHW081620220526
45468CB00010B/2955
9781983409660